DESK CALENDAR 2024
VAN GOGH PAINTINGS

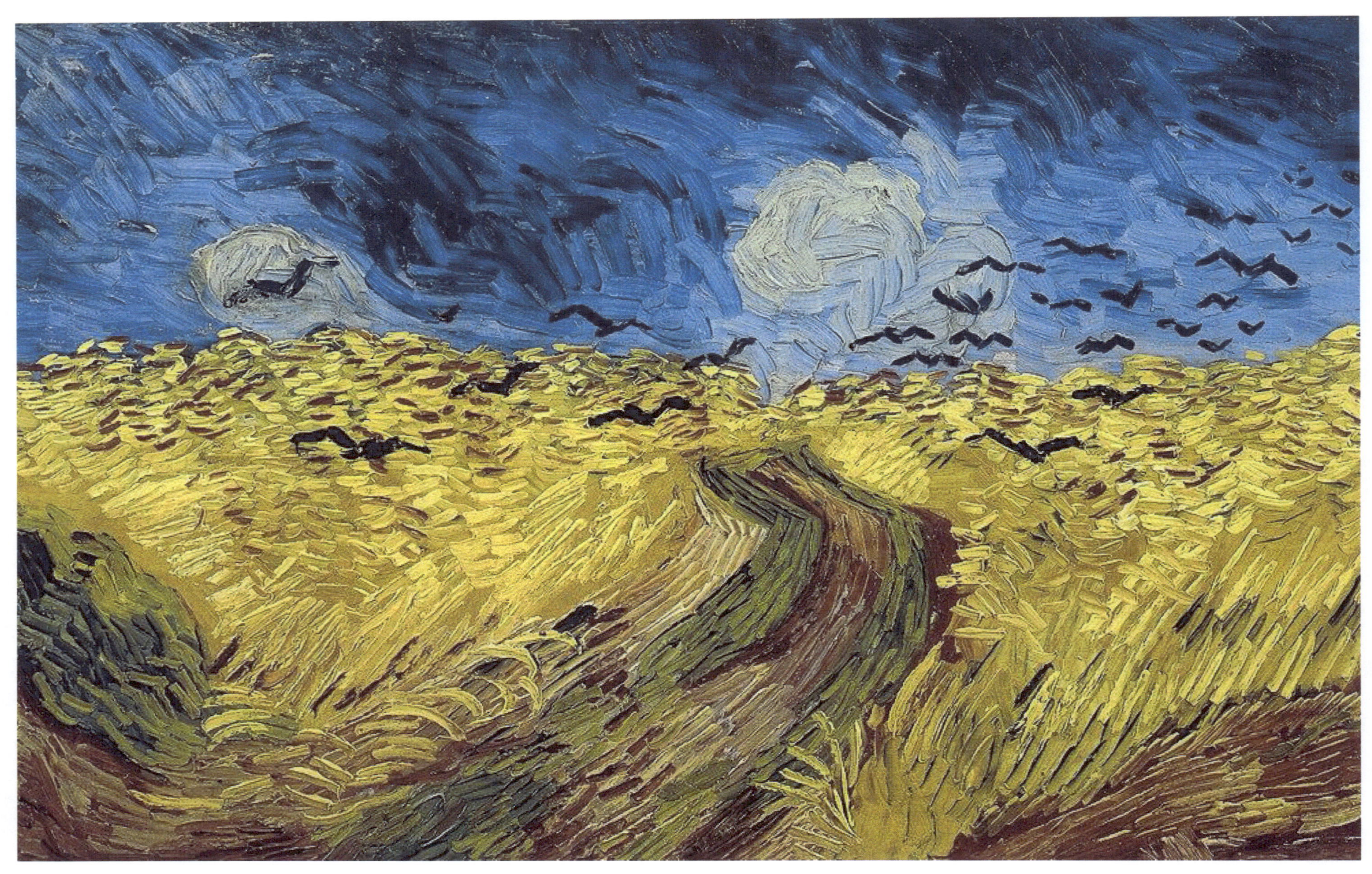

Wheatfield with Crows, 1890 by Vincent Van Gogh

GOALS

NOTES

TO DO LIST

JANUARY | 2024

SUNDAY	MONDAY	TUESDAY	WEDNESDAY	THURSDAY	FRIDAY	SATURDAY
	1 New Year's Day	2	2	4	5	6
7	8	9	10	11	12	13
14	15 Martin Luther King Jr. Day	16	17	18	19	20
21	22	23	24	25	26	27
28	29	30	31			

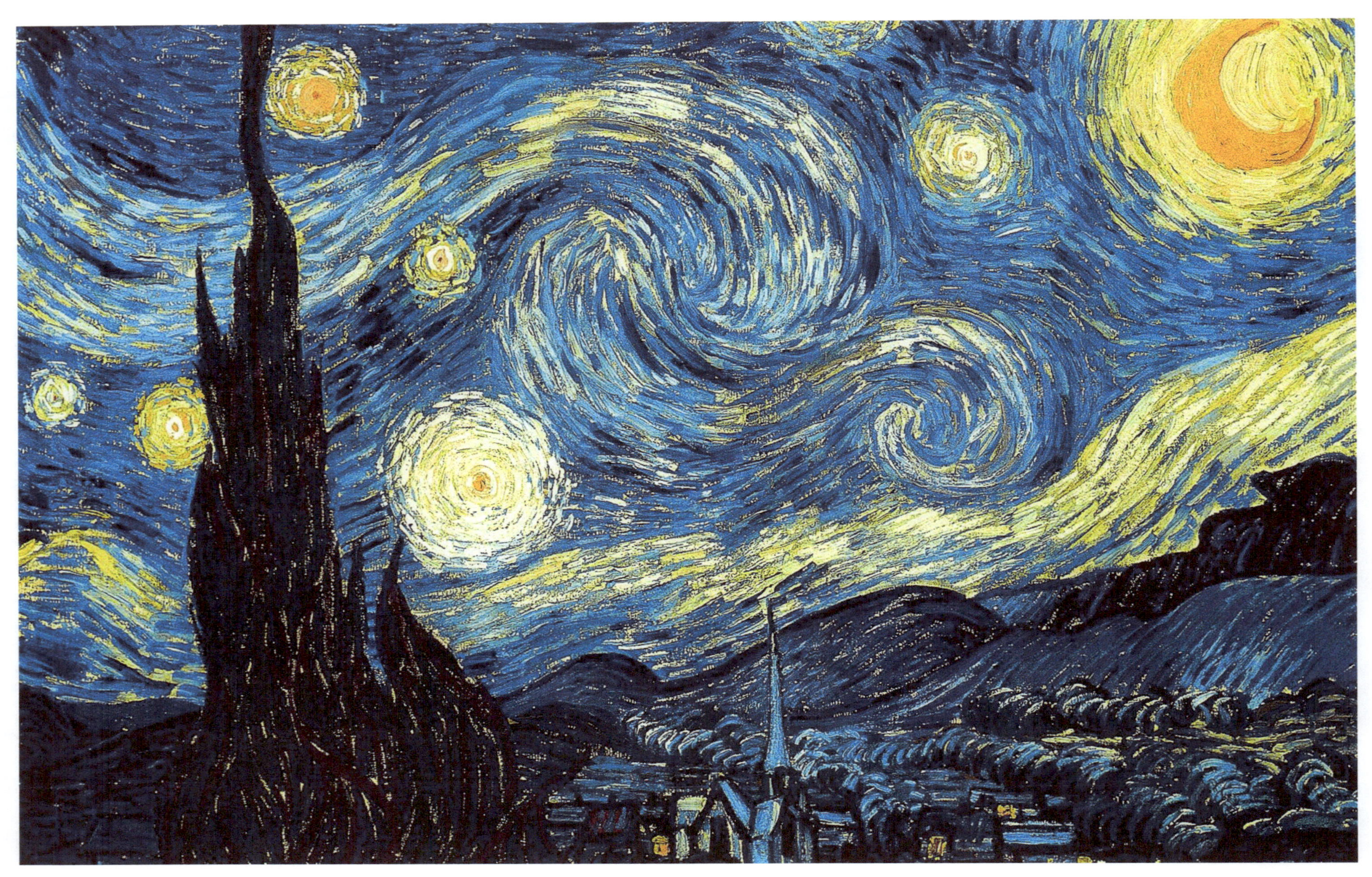

THE STARRY NIGHT, 1889 BY VINCENT VAN GOGH

GOALS

NOTES

TO DO LIST

FEBRUARY | 2024

SUNDAY	MONDAY	TUESDAY	WEDNESDAY	THURSDAY	FRIDAY	SATURDAY
				1	2 Columbus Day	3
4	5	6	7	8	9	10
11	12 Lincoln's Birthday	13	14 Valentine's Day	15	16	17
18	19 President's Day	20	21	22	23	24
25	26	27	28	29		

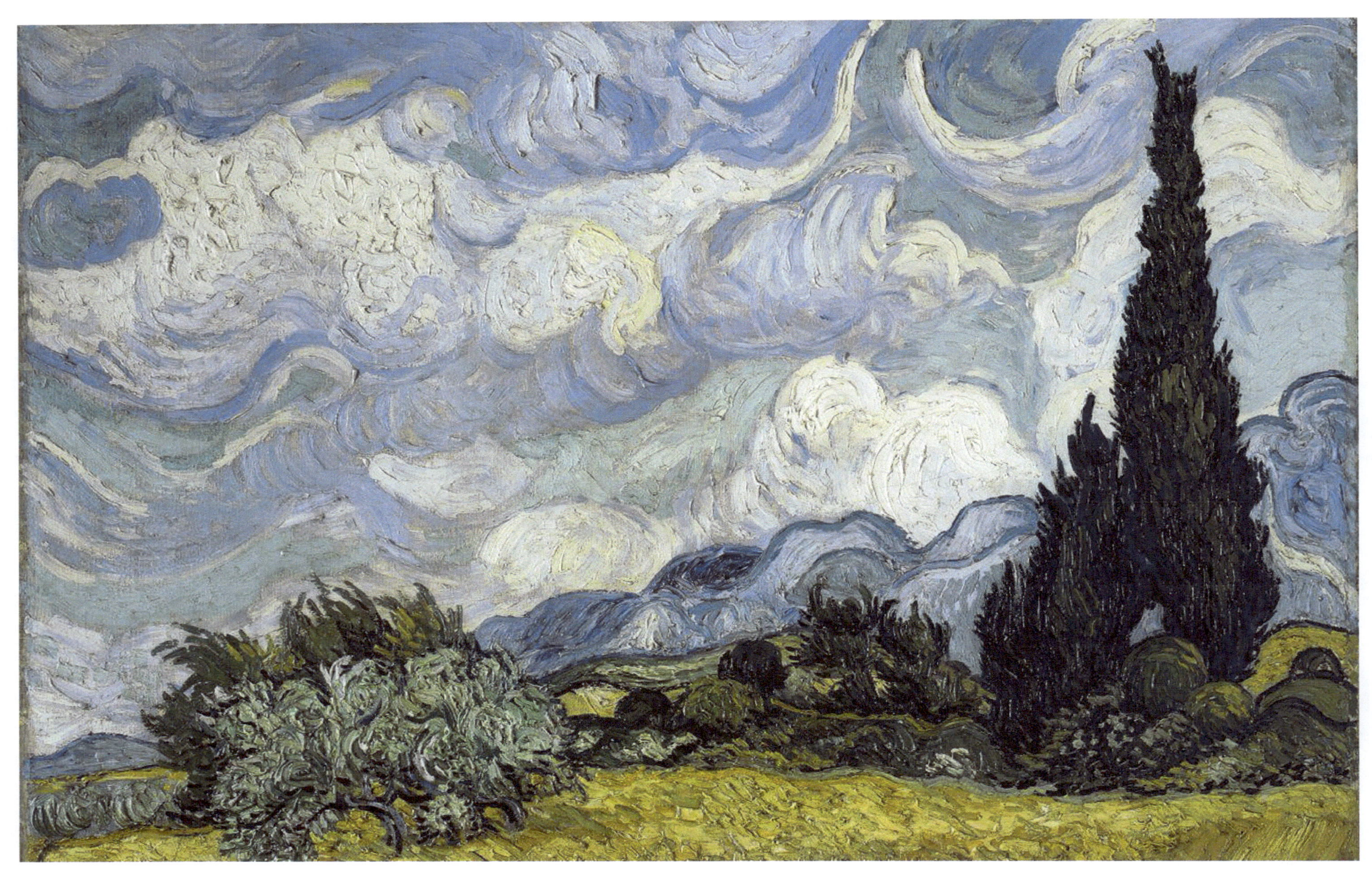

WHEATFIELD WITH CYPRESSES, 1889 BY VINCENT VAN GOGH

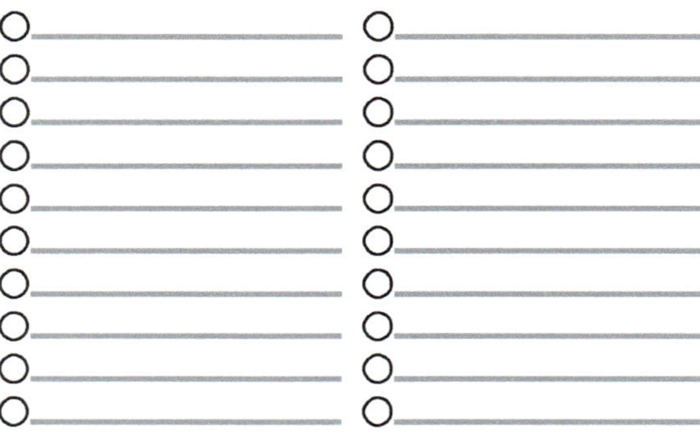

MARCH | 2024

SUNDAY	MONDAY	TUESDAY	WEDNESDAY	THURSDAY	FRIDAY	SATURDAY
					1	2
3	4	5	6	7	8	9
10 Daylight Saving Time Begins	11	12	13	14	15	16
17 St. Patrick's Day	18	19 Spring Begins	20	21	22	23
24 Palm Sunday	25	26	27	28	29 Good Friday	30
31 Easter						

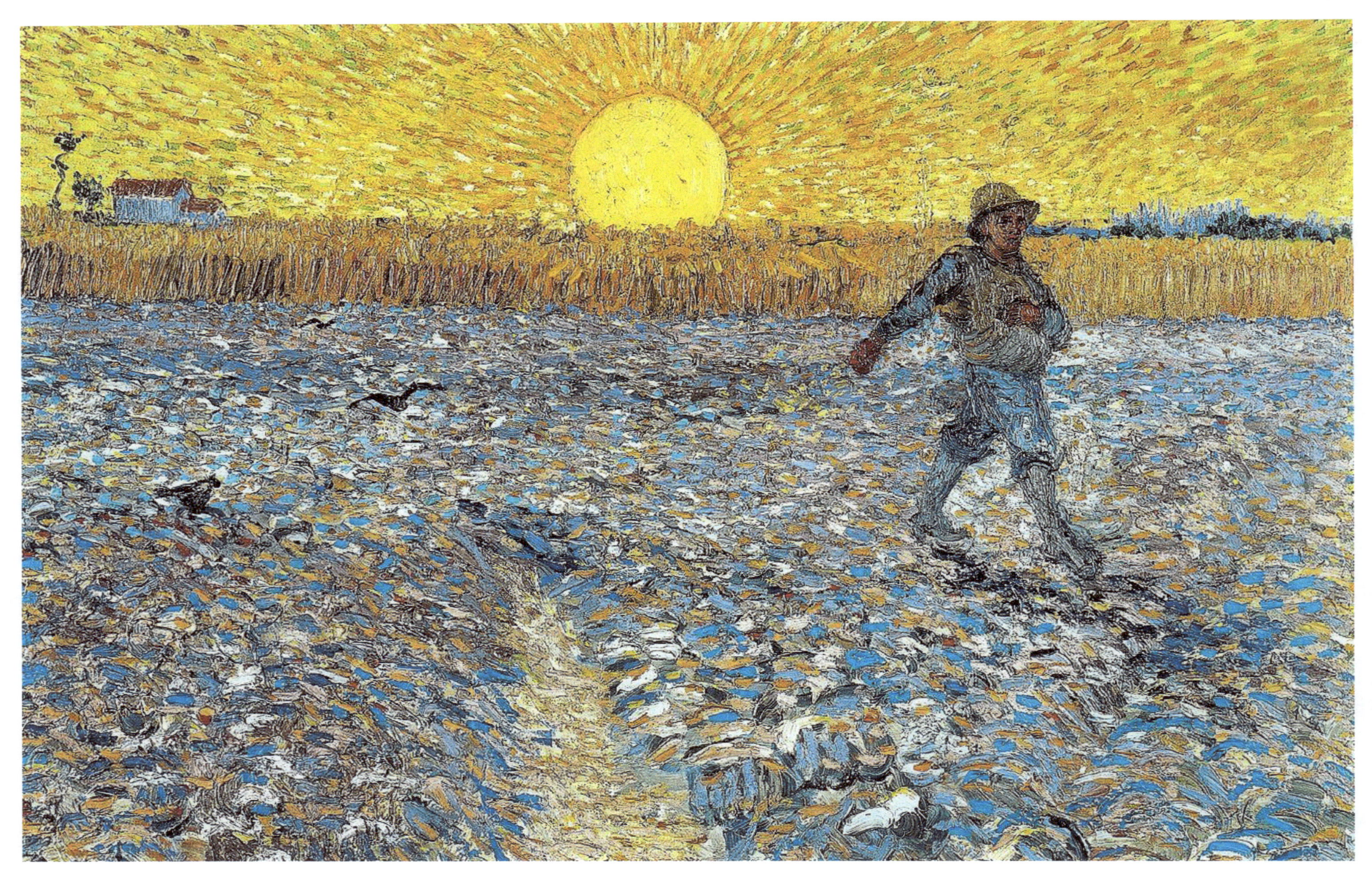

THE SOWER, 1888 BY VINCENT VAN GOGH

GOALS

NOTES

TO DO LIST

APRIL | 2024

SUNDAY	MONDAY	TUESDAY	WEDNESDAY	THURSDAY	FRIDAY	SATURDAY
	1 April Fool's Day	2	3	4	5	6
7	8	9	10	11	12	13
14	15	16	17	18	19	20
21	22 Earth Day	23	24	25	26	27
28	29	30				

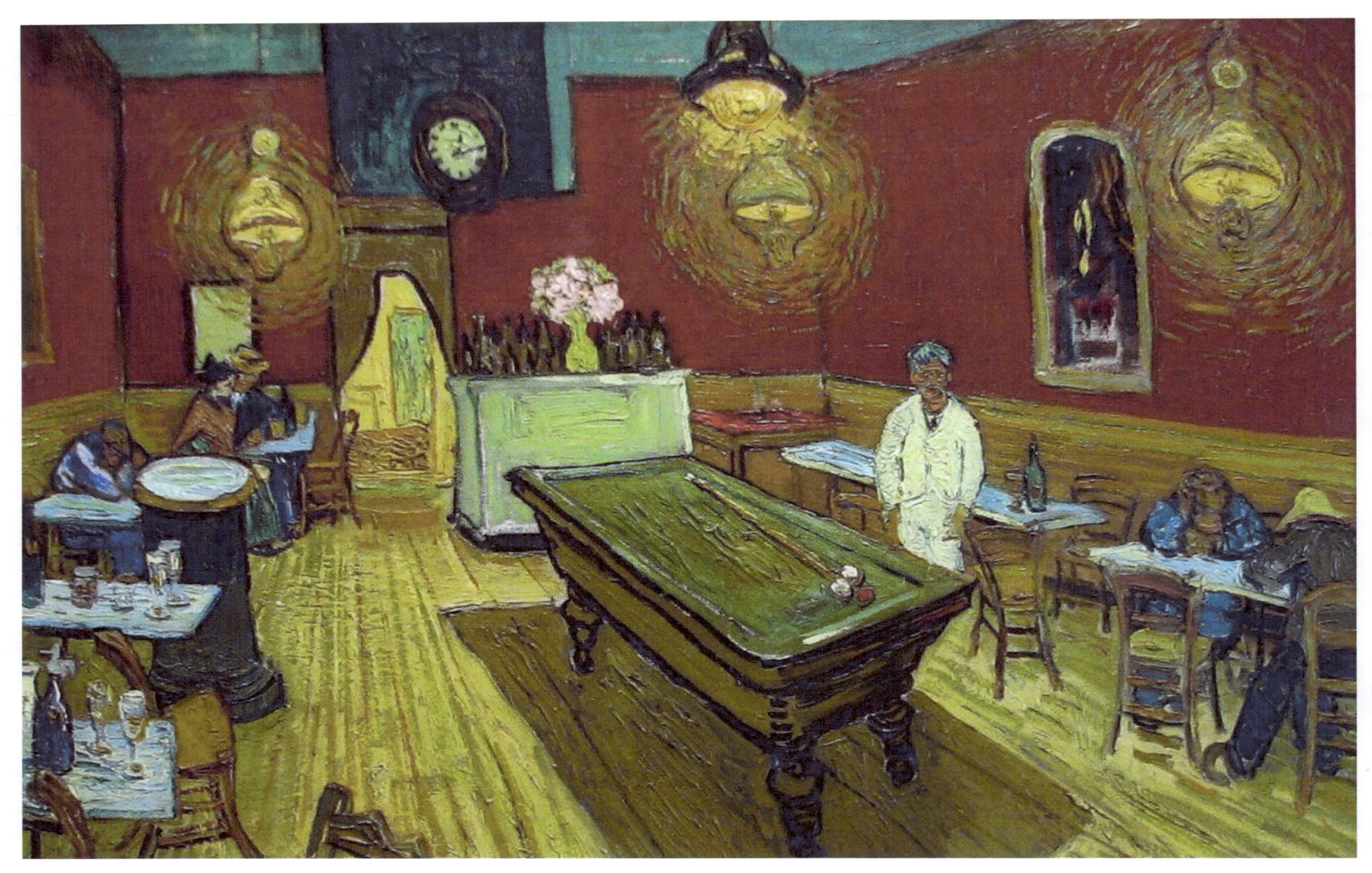

THE NIGHT CAFE, 1888 BY VINCENT VAN GOGH

GOALS

NOTES

TO DO LIST

MAY | 2024

SUNDAY	MONDAY	TUESDAY	WEDNESDAY	THURSDAY	FRIDAY	SATURDAY
			1	2	3	4
5 Cinco' de Mayo	6	7	8	9	10	11
12 Mother's Day	13	14	15	16	17	18 Armed Forces Day
19	20	21 Veterans Day	22	23	24	25
26	27 Memorial Day	28	29	30	31	

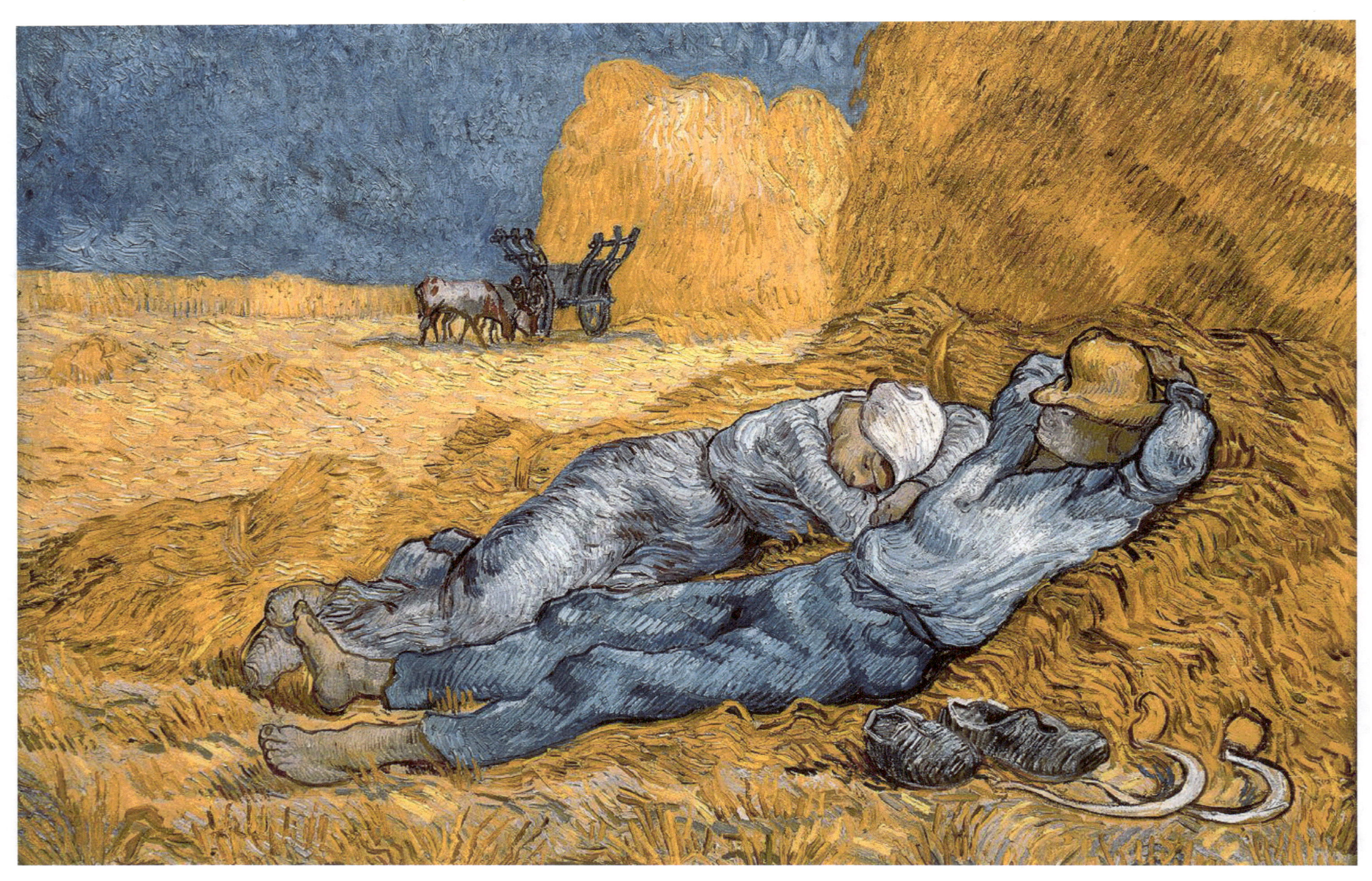

Noon Rest At Work, 1890 by Vincent Van Gogh

June | 2024

SUNDAY	MONDAY	TUESDAY	WEDNESDAY	THURSDAY	FRIDAY	SATURDAY
						1
2	3	4	5	6	7	8
9	10	11	12	13	14 Flag Day	15
16 Father's Day	17	18	19 Juneteenth	20 Summer Begins	21	22
23	24	25	26	27	28	29
30						

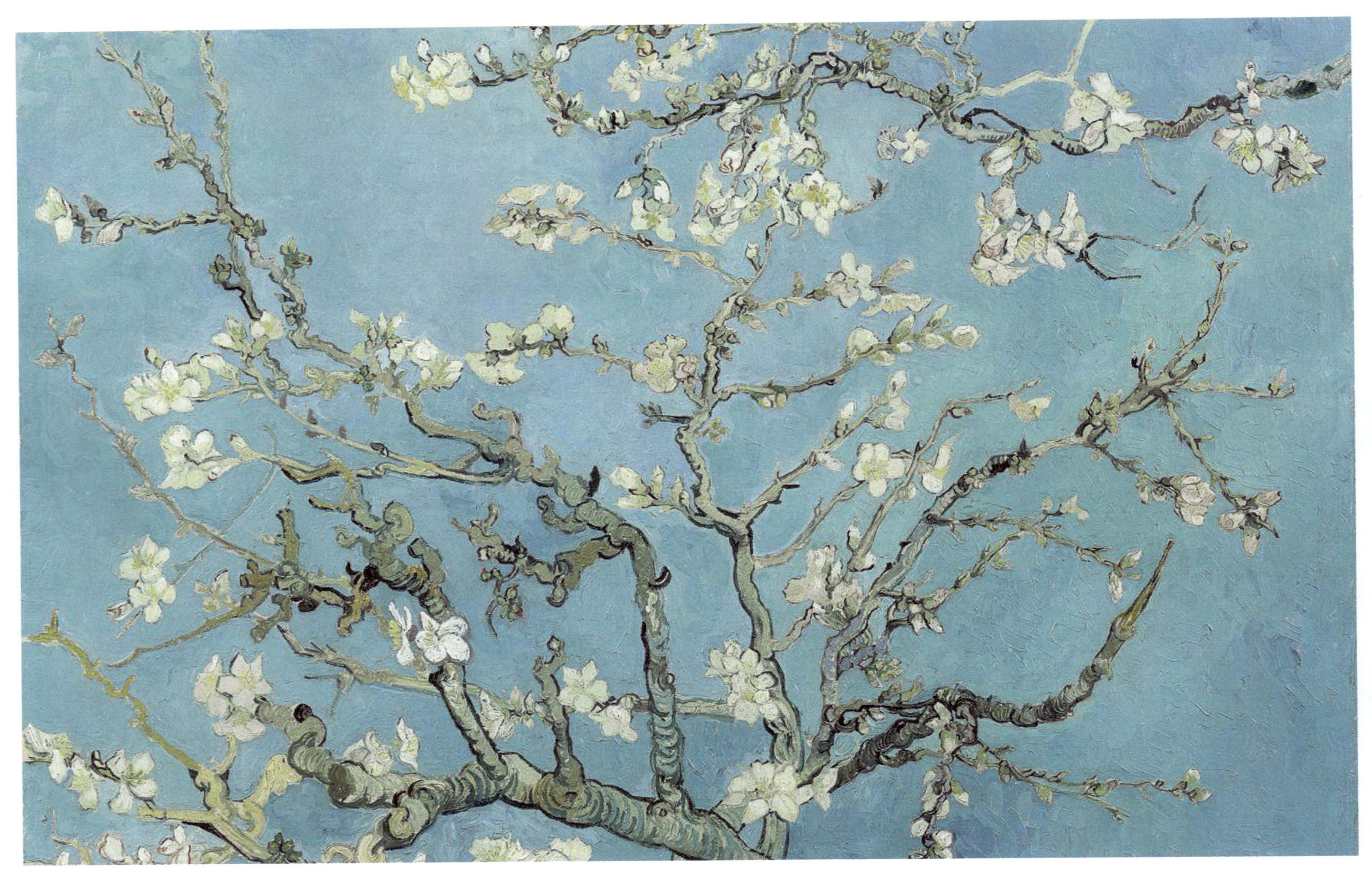

ALMOND BLOSSOMS, 1890 BY VINCENT VAN GOGH

GOALS

NOTES

TO DO LIST

JULY | 2024

SUNDAY	MONDAY	TUESDAY	WEDNESDAY	THURSDAY	FRIDAY	SATURDAY
	1	2	3	4 Independence Day	5	6
7	8	9	10	11	12	13
14	15	16	17	18	19	20
21	22	23	24	25	26	27
28	29	30	31			

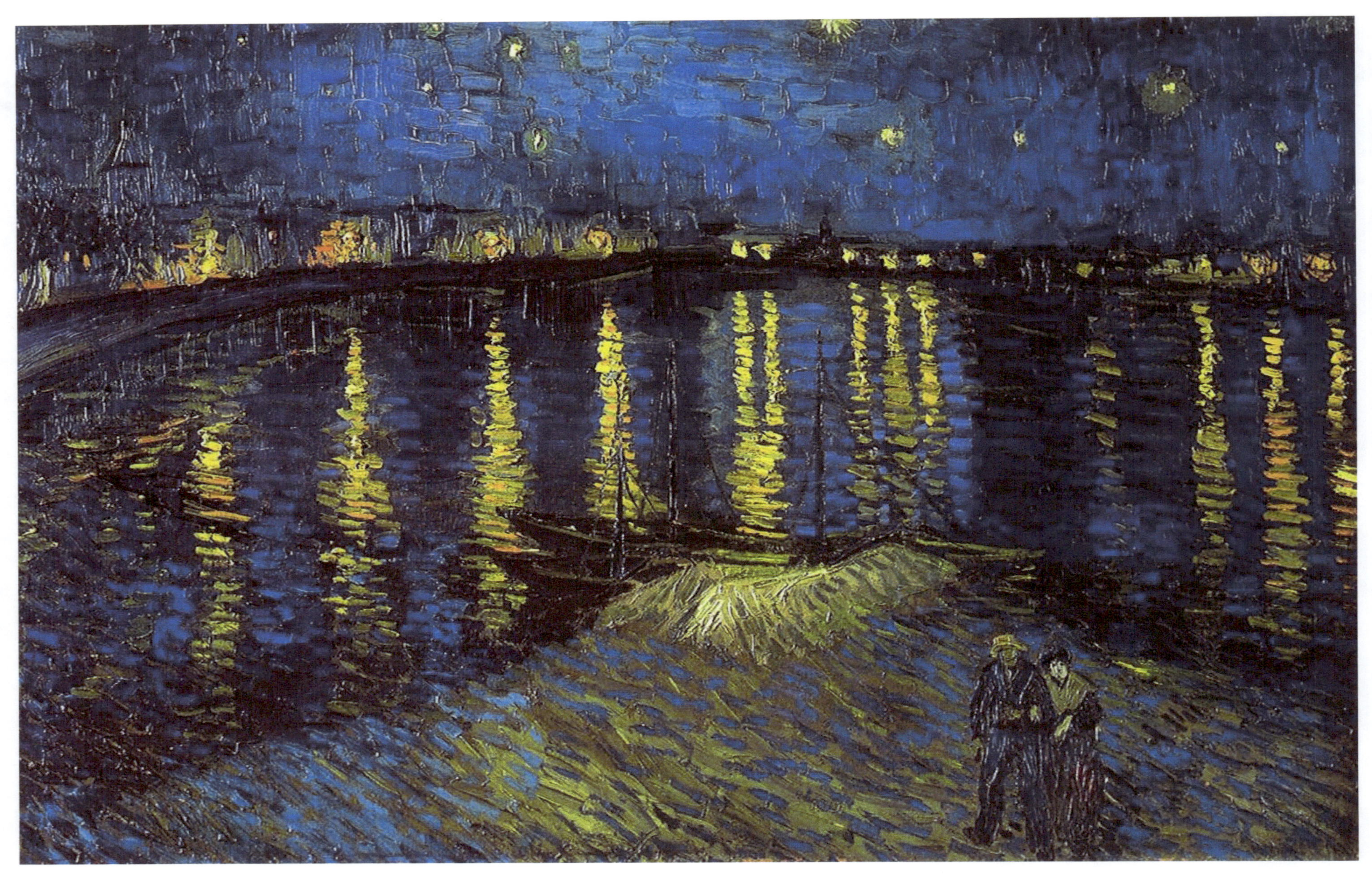

Starry Night Over The Rhone, 1888 by Vincent Van Gogh

GOALS

NOTES

TO DO LIST

AUGUST | 2024

SUNDAY	MONDAY	TUESDAY	WEDNESDAY	THURSDAY	FRIDAY	SATURDAY
				1	2	3
4	5	6	7	8	9	10
11	12	13	14	15	16	17
18	19	20	21	22	23	24
25	26	27	28	29	30	31

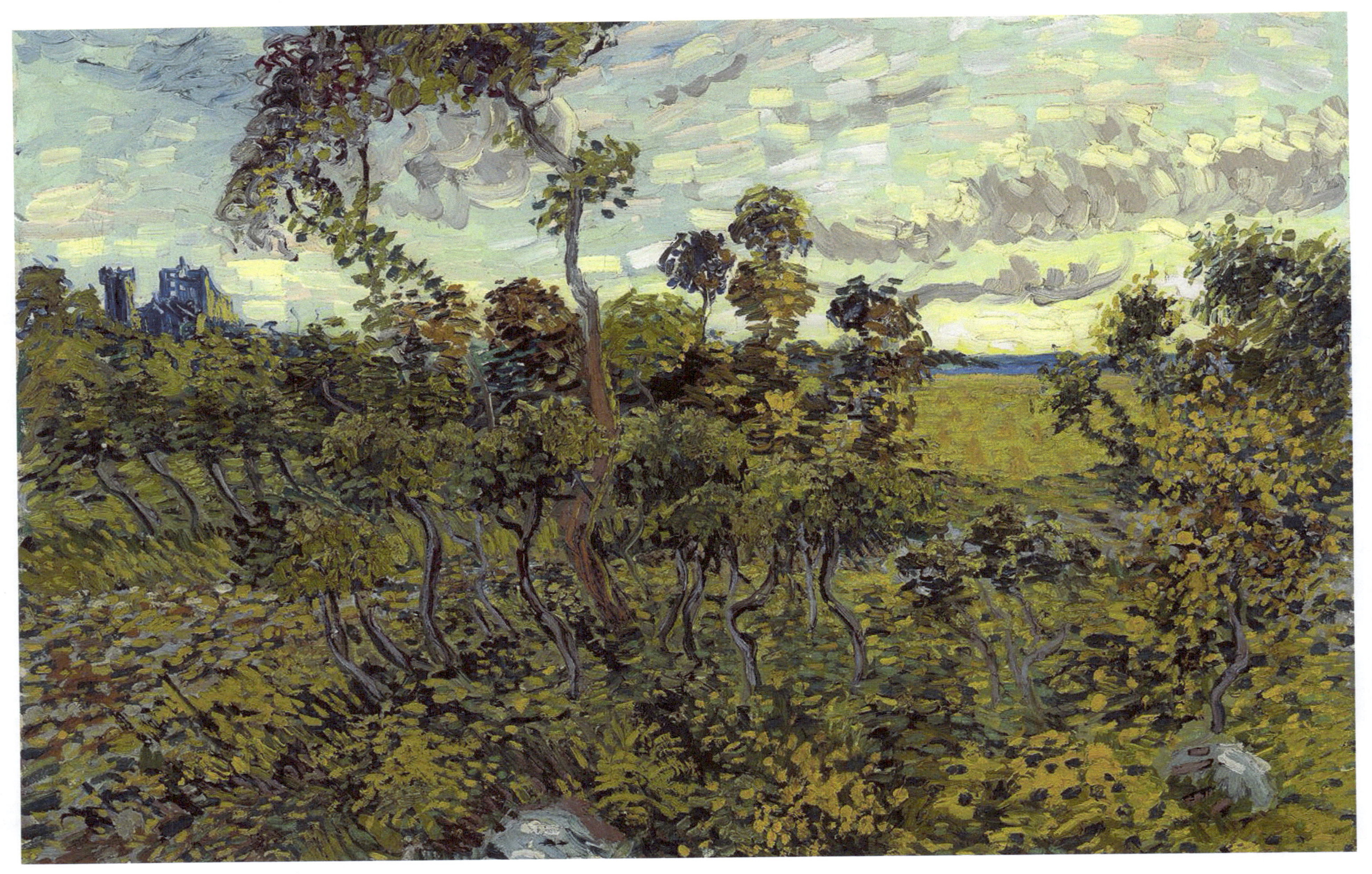

THE RED VINEYARD AT ARLES, 1888 BY VINCENT VAN GOGH

GOALS

NOTES

TO DO LIST

September | 2024

SUNDAY	MONDAY	TUESDAY	WEDNESDAY	THURSDAY	FRIDAY	SATURDAY
1	2 Labor Day	3	4	5	6	7
8 Grandparents Day	9	10	11	12	13	14
15	16	17	18	19	20	21
22 Autumn Begins	23	24	25	26	27	28
29	30					

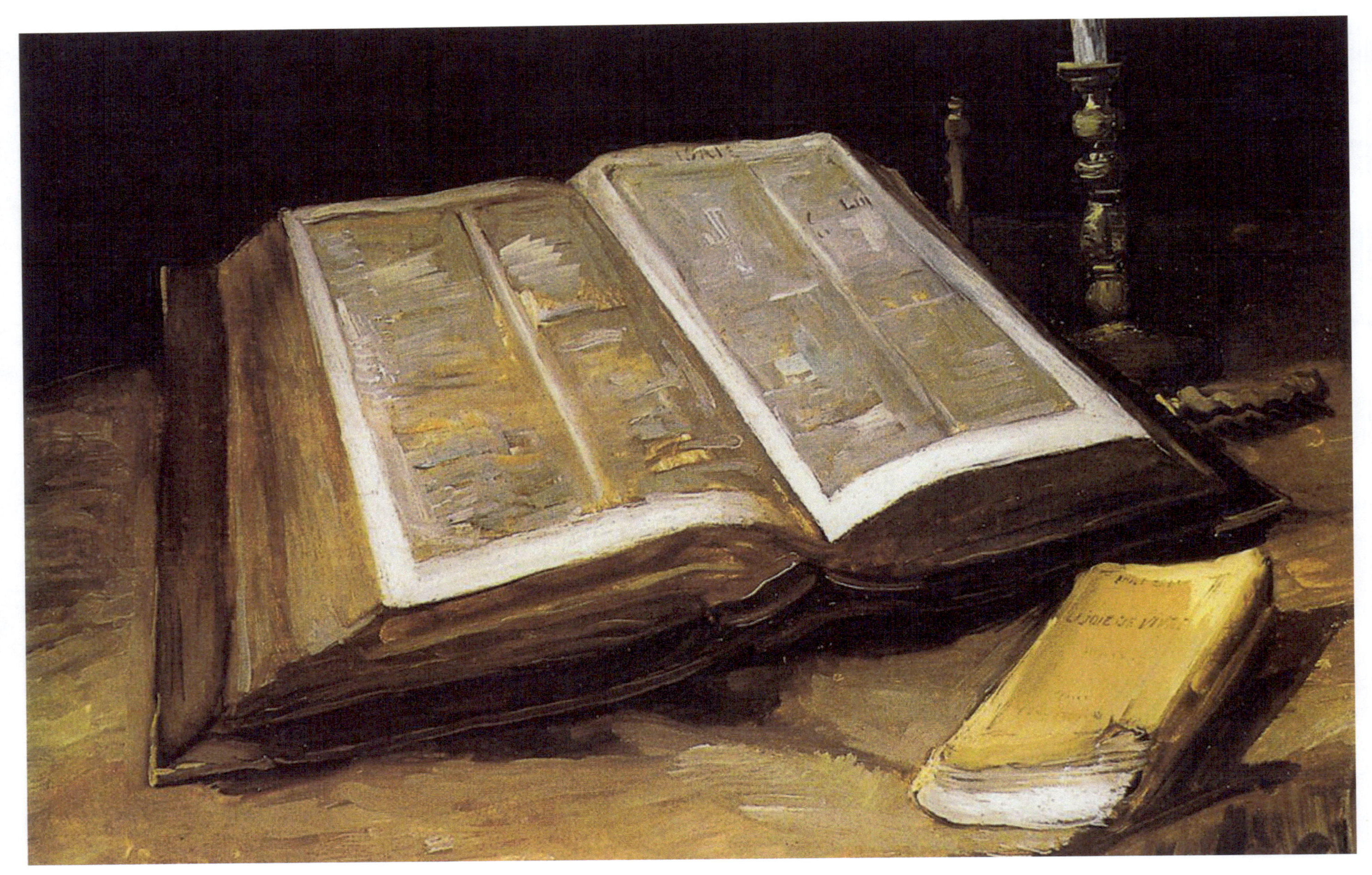

STILL LIFE WITH BIBLE, 1885 BY VINCENT VAN GOGH

GOALS

NOTES

TO DO LIST

October | 2024

SUNDAY	MONDAY	TUESDAY	WEDNESDAY	THURSDAY	FRIDAY	SATURDAY
		1	2 Rosh Hashanah	3	4	5
6	7	8	9	10	11 Yom Kippur	12
13	14 Indigenous Peoples' Day	15	16	17	18	19
20	21	22	23	24	25	26
27	28	29	30	31 Halloween		

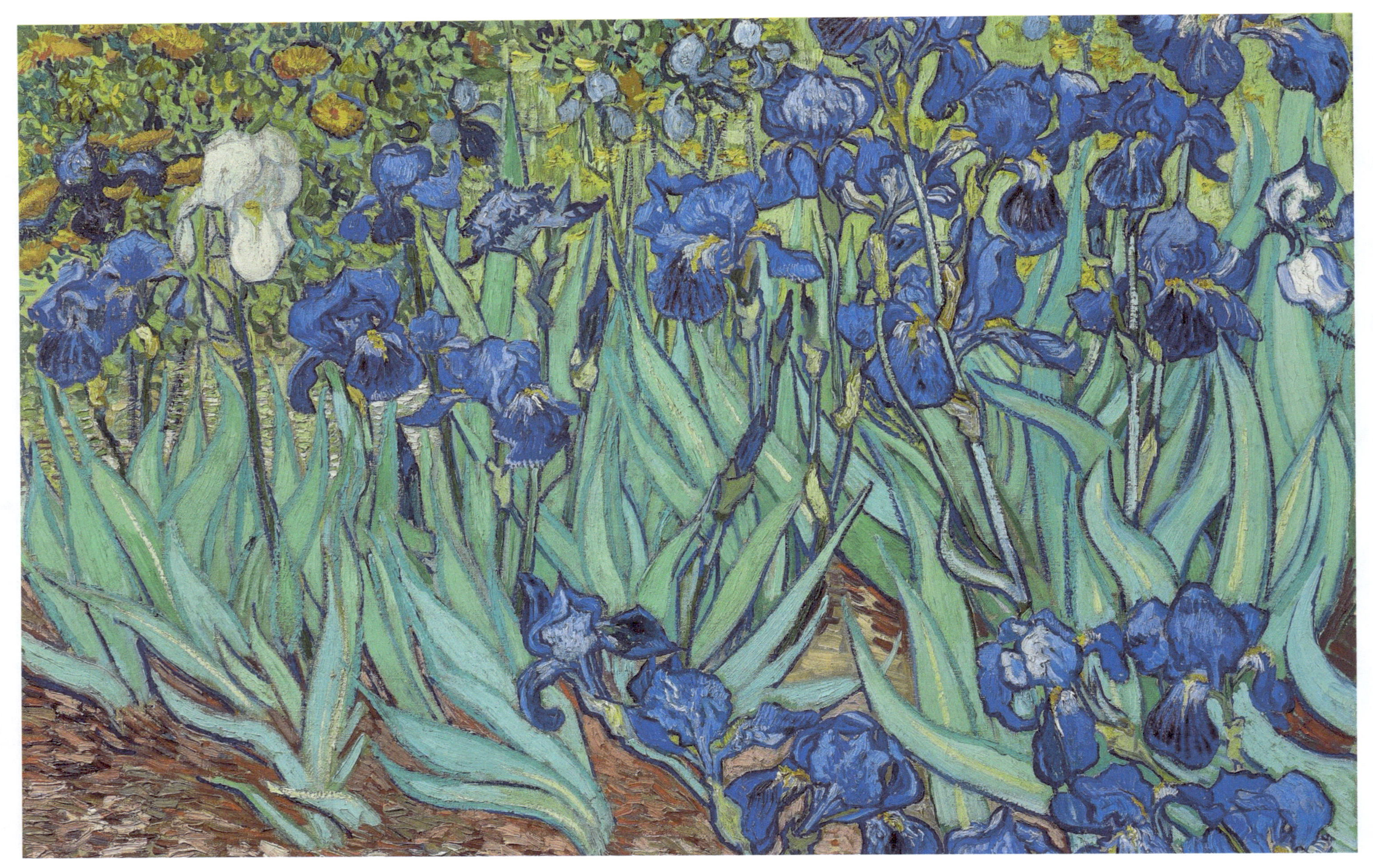

IRISES, 1889 BY VINCENT VAN GOGH

<table>
<tr><td>

GOALS

NOTES

TO DO LIST

</td><td>

November | 2024

SUNDAY	MONDAY	TUESDAY	WEDNESDAY	THURSDAY	FRIDAY	SATURDAY
					1	2
3 Daylight Saving (end)	4	5	6	7	8	9
10	11 Veterans Day	12	13	14	15	16
17	18	19	20	21	22	23
24	25	26	27	28 Thanksgiving	29	30

</td></tr>
</table>

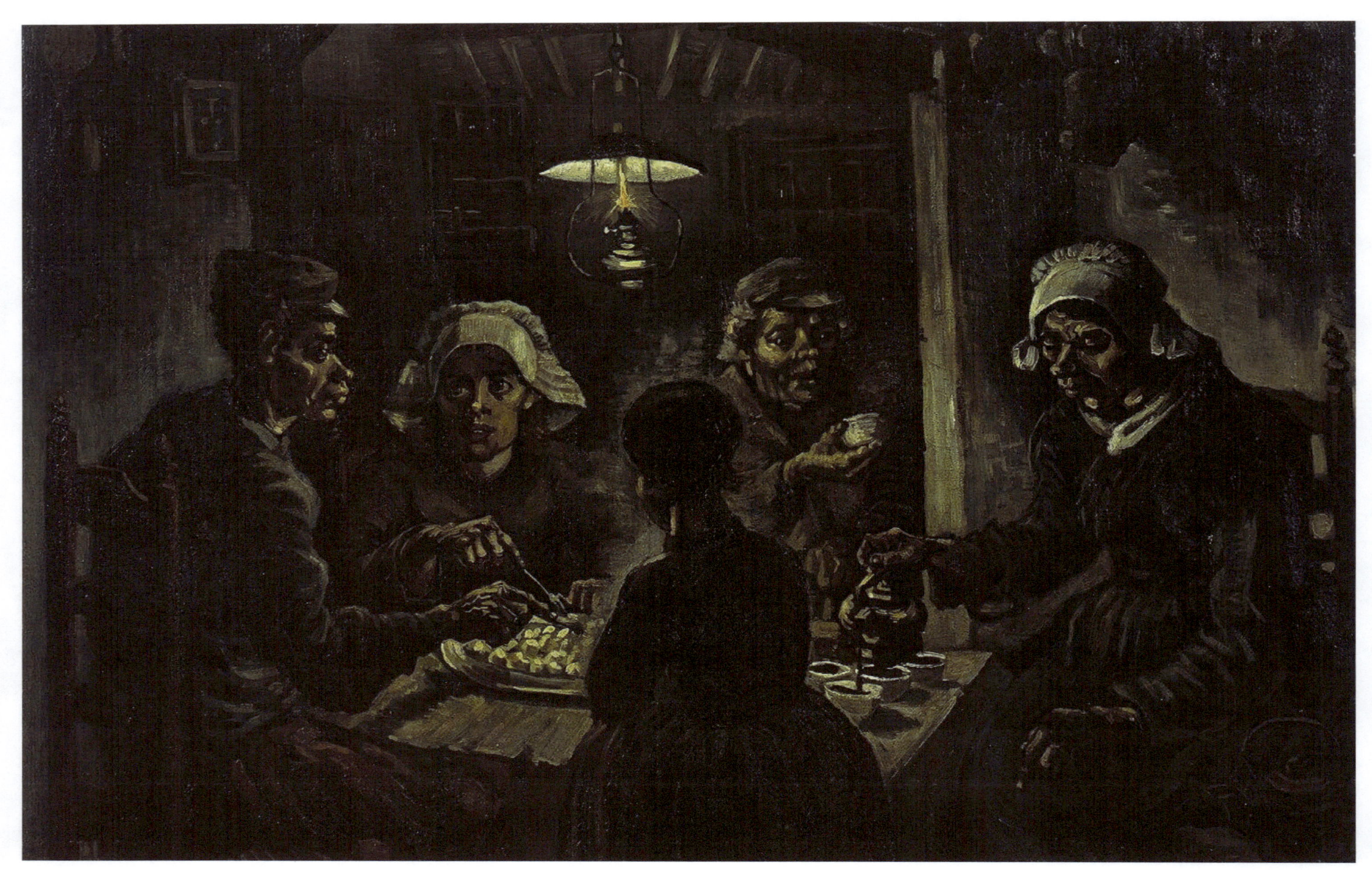

The Potato Eaters, 1885 by Vincent Van Gogh

DECEMBER | 2024

SUNDAY	MONDAY	TUESDAY	WEDNESDAY	THURSDAY	FRIDAY	SATURDAY
1	2	3	4	5	6	7
8	9	10	11	12	13	14
15	16	17	18	19	20	21 Winter Begins
22	23	24	25 Hanukkah Begins Christmas Day	26 Kwanzaa begins	27	28
29	30	31 New Year's Eve				